BLUES LIKE THE TIDES

BLUES LIKE THE TIDES

by

Stephen C. Shaw

To Ronnie
May the
tides be with
you
Steve Shaw

Parisburg Publishing

2010

Cover photo of Stephen C. Shaw's artwork
taken by Patricia Hutchins
Cover's painting and all graphic/line drawings by Stephen C. Shaw

First Edition

First Printing

Parisburg Publishing
www.parisburgpublishing.com

ISBN: 9781453638927

(A createspace project)

Dedicated to
John Sebastian
who sold me my first guitar
and whose love for tidal blues
has inspired me
for over 50 years

CONTENTS

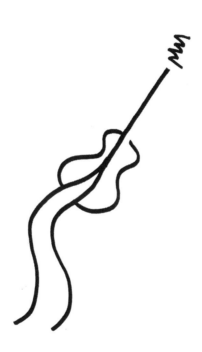

PREFACE

Blues Like the Tides consists of four Chapters and a Coda, as follows:

CHAPTER ONE: A GIFT OF THE RIVER

Herodotus, the "Father of History," called Egypt the gift of a river. The land of the Delta blues is also a gift of a river, not the Egyptian Nile, of course, but the American Mississippi. The Delta blues have deep roots which thrive in river-gifted soil.

The blues have been derogatively called "the Devil's music," but this stiff-necked judgment misses an essential point. For the blues assert one of the best qualities of true religion: empathy for the poor and ostracized. How do you hold on to your dignity in a world full of harsh, demeaning condescension? You sing the blues. That is the gift the blues bring to the exploited, the repressed, and the defiant ones who fight against dehumanization with every blues breath.

CHAPTER TWO: BLUES ARCHAEOLOGISTS

The next chapter shows the influence of the classic American bluesmen on modern songwriters, especially those in England, where the blues revival of the '60's reawakened Americans to their own musical heritage.

The Chapter focuses on modern songs written in the blues idiom. Many classic blues were created during the Depression, and depression is certainly at the heart of the blues. But so is therapeutic catharsis. You fall in a ditch. Everybody passes you by. The blues pick you up. The blues do not promise certain judgment, but unexpected mercy.

This is also the Chapter which draws an analogy between the blues and archaeology. Upon discovering some shards of a buried blues lyric, a modern blues man or woman must use as much creativity as possible to piece them together. Modern "songcathers" must dig down through several layers of musical soil in order to find the real down-home blues. We've encountered this fertile soil before: it is a gift of the river.

CHAPTER THREE: THIRTEEN LUCKY POETS

This chapter links American blues to American poetry. We examine how thirteen poets, one to match each star in the original American flag, handle blues themes. A poet turns lucky whenever he or she can come to grips with melancholy through honest poetic expression, honest expression powerful enough to exorcise what used to be called "the blue devils." What if poets like Emily Dickinson and Robert Lowell had written poems based on themes found in classical blues? The poems in this Chapter explore this premise thirteen times.

CHAPTER FOUR: ZENCHANTMENT AND WORD JAZZ

This Chapter examines the Beat Poetry Movement of the 'fifties. The Chapter explores the blues and jazz roots of Kerouac, Ginsberg, and Burroughs. From the poetry of the blues emerges the poetry of American Bohemia, a reaction against uniforms and uniformity, regulation and regimentation, rigidity and the *rigor mortis* of a society clinging to a Puritanical humorlessness.

The ability to find creativity in a dull world of quiet suburban desperation—that is another great gift of the blues. The blue devils of conformity are banished by Zenchantment. Beat-tific poems enliven and enrich standardized thinking.

CODA: WHAT IT MEANS?

Lastly comes a Coda written in a prose style derived from the inventiveness of jazz improvisation. In this section, musical riddles ask which instrument is being played in a jazz combo. Once again the theme of mercy arises, but, as the down-and-out bluesman puts it, do we really know what it means?

# # #

Like mercy, the quality of the blues is not strained.

The real gift of the blues is their way of showing us how to keep the lifeforce vibrant and merciful.

Tides and taxes—they notoriously wait for no one. But the blues love perpetual motion. Blues *like* the tides.

And, the blues also have the uncanny ability to handle emotional taxation in truly unexpected ways.

Steve Shaw
Harrisburg, PA
June 2010

CHAPTER ONE

A GIFT OF THE RIVER

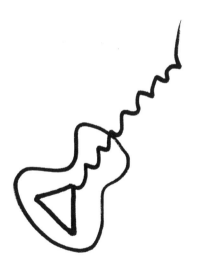

PART ONE: THE BLUES FABRIC

THEREFORE, GO FORTH
AND MULTIPLY THE BLUES

The blues is the only poetry
allowed to an exploited sharecropper.

No Marlowe, no Shakespeare,
No Shelley, no Whitman.

no moan for Faust,
no King Lear sorrow song,
No prison song
for a shackled Prometheus,
no bluenote in the leavings
of grass.

But plenty of deep feeling
for lost emancipation,
for the crushed worker
at the bottom of the pyramid,
for your soul on sale
in the company store.

The sharecropper's blues
is the sung poetry
of the unsung poet...

A GIFT OF THE RIVER

Who does not know
Harry Smith?

That freewheeling
honorary anthropologist
of hidden connections?

The Harry Smith Anthology
on Folkways Records
drove me to the wasteland.

Actually I drove myself,
in an old De Soto,
named for an old explorer,
who discovered the unexpected
deep in the Mississippi Delta.

We— me and De Soto,
and my imaginary friend—
took off from Morningside Heights
for destinations like Yazoo,
Concordia Island, Ruleville,
and Mound Bayou.

We were songcatchers in search
of a landscape shaped
by Old Man River,
who still keeps rolling along
to the melancholy rhythm
of the blues.

\# \# \#

In many ways the trip
was a real gift,
and I could not fail to recall
how Herodotus described Egypt:
"...an acquired country,
the gift of a river."

\# \# \#

On the way, I fancied
I had Harry Smith with me
in the passenger seat
of my old explorer car.

We had a lively discussion
about the rich creativity
of poverty-slapped barrel-housers,
powerful neglected bluesmen
who enlightened the vinyl
of Harry Smith's record collection.

It was uncanny
how Harry knew my own
convictions so well.

It was as if I were
in dialog with myself...

"It really gets my scapegoat,"
I heard Harry excitedly yell out,
"We have Jonathan Edwards
and Longfellow in our anthologies,
and Robert Frost, and Emily Dickinson,
but not a scrap of Blind Lemon Jefferson."

"Too blind for Braille,
too black for white pages."

I was a lot more clever
in my imagination than
in real life.

The De Soto coughed
and seemed to agree.

"Damn straight."
Harry continued,
"Just look at the first line
of *Cymbeline,*
where Shakespeare says:

You do not see a man,
but frowns."

I knew that first line well.
Who but an English major
would ever read such obscurities
so determinedly they could light up
an obscure soul?

"Now, compare that
with Charlie Patton's phrase,
face all over frowns."

"I know, it's uncanny."

It was one of my favorite words.

"Or Blind Lemon's
*I feel like jumping
through the keyhole
in your door.*
I tell you, that beats Longfellow
any day of the week."

"I love Blind Lemon.
Remember *I wanna go home,
but I ain't got sufficient clothes*?"

"Of course, I always felt
sufficient made that line."

"You're soooo right."

"And a poet like that
not even allowed
the back of the bus
of anthologies
of American literature."

# # #

The next day I made it
to Belzoni, Mississippi,
intending to record
a contemporary blues poet
who would never be anthologized.

Harry Smith's indignation
was all over my
recording heads.

And, in my own head,
there was another
of the un-anthologized
blues lines he loved to quote:
*I can look through muddy water
till I see dry land.*

And, here in the flatlands
of the Delta, I knew *I* could.

And I could also swear that
that Old Man River,
with his face all over frowns,
give me and Harry Smith
a secret nod before
he just kept rolling along...

FLOOD'S THE NEW BULLY

The flood's the new bully of this town,
ain't no one here to knock that bully down.

Frogs jumped high when the levee broke.
Two in the Ark, all the others croaked.

Them levees moaned, like dogs in packs.
Trains do the dog paddle on flooded tracks.

Noah got seasick when the water rolled.
Two chained black men down in the hold.

BLACK RAINBOW

Flooded

Noah's insides were flooded
with the blues.
He was the first
to drink in the backwater
which would turn the Delta's stomach.

Before and After

Before the '27 flood,
black codes stole the light.
After the '27 flood,
black codes stole the light.
You might as well
photograph the rainbow
without color film.

NO TROUBLE FOR THE CHANDELIERS

Black water and Black Codes
sure do make quite a pair.
And blackened law, like backwater,
leaves its stain most everywhere.

After the flood,
the Red Cross responded
quickly.

But the federal money
went mostly to the fat pockets
of the fat white pants
of the fat white men
who doled out
the lean black laws.

All the cold and howling night,
the restless backwater moaned.
When backwater comes night-riding,
you feel its hoof kick all your bones.

Some of the homeless
were drafted into rebuilding
the levees.

One or two protested.

But not for long...

They were hit
over their uppity heads,
and their cracked bodies
were efficiently shoveled
into wet cement.

When your plantation's high on the hill,
floodwater don't trouble the chandeliers.
That flood water don't hurt nobody,
'cepting them that sees and hears.

THE BLUES FABRIC

Dark heads bob in the white field.

They weave a winding sheet
as old as the Pharaoh's.

Of crops, Pharaoh Cotton
is the most perverse,
scarring the fingers of pickers
with its prickly bolls.

After work,
some still found time
to play a home-made guitar,
even though it made
their fingers bleed
even more.

For them, the music
does a lot more good
than a cotton bandage.

DOWSERS

The rough and tumble growl
of the Father of the Delta Blues
had a tender side.

Charlie Patton's voice came from
the deepest well in his heart.

It was a heart in the right place
for sweet water.

His blues were dowsers
during the driest spell.

SHAKING HANDS WITH FATHER TIME

I was laid up in an iron jail,
thought I could hear my good gal call.
But the dumb thing I was chained to
sure wasn't no crystal ball.

"Well, good morning, now Judge,
what might be my fine?"
"Mercy, mercy, you poor boy,
you'll be shaking hands with Father Time."

And now I sure wish Mr. Charlie
never made me fight that night.
Far as a blind judge can see,
a good ol' boy is always right...

Now I'm all laid up in stir,
chained up like some mutt.
And the blues keep on a rattlin',
like some chain inside my gut.

So, I'm laid up in jail,
thought I could hear my good gal call.
And it sure wasn't nothin'
but the rats singing in the wall.

BURDENED SHAFTS OF LIGHT

The burdened shafts of light
cast shadows of the bars
on the nasty floor.

Even the sun, he thought,
can't break free
of a barred window.

LOST HOMELAND

Skip James—
what a long history
that man's fingers had.

They sought out
haunting melodies on taut strings,
and then again on the broken-tusked keys
of a stained piano.

They made me think of Chinaberry roots
growing deeper and deeper south
to seek out their lost homeland...

My mother used to tell me:
"Eat up, there are people
starving in China."

I'm all grown up now,
and, Mom, I still haven't been there.

But I have been to places at home
where people seek out their roots
to keep from starving.

PART TWO: BLUES IN A FLAT LAND

TELL FROM A LITTLE

*"I can tell from a little
just what a whole lot means."
--Furry Lewis*

I inherited my father's store,
and I made enough money
to live well in the most southern part
of the Christian promised land.

I had a spaniel back then,
and I used to love
how he'd stick his head
out the window of my Terraplane.

He'd happily relish how
the wind made angel wings
out of his furried ears.

# # #

In my town of Ruleville,
there was an old black woman,
kind and solid and honest.

My father taught me
to love generosity
as much as the Torah,
so I decided to hire her,
and pay her a generous salary...

I knew I had violated a local taboo,
but my father taught me
to love mercy more than taboos.

We were the only game in town,
that is, if you were white
and wanted to buy
the goods you needed
to make a living.

# # #

At first, they accepted her,
and, besides, she was friendly,
and treated them better
than they would have treated
a Reformed Jew,
like my father, the eternal stranger
in their familiar land.

But we weren't strangers
any more, and, besides,
we were the tolerated Jews
who had a lot of the essential
stuff they needed to survive.

My best clerk would
carefully package up
their hammers, and black nails,
and black shoes for their mules
and kids...

And they had to drop
their money into
that kind, black hand,
the one which always
gave them back honest change.

# # #

But I paid for hiring her,
in that land so familiar
to the narrow-eyed
and hard-hearted.

They killed my spaniel.

They left his body
on the welcome mat
set out by my father.

BLUES IN A FLAT LAND

What the paddle wheel
is to the River,
the blues are
to the flat land.

So, it takes a work gang to moan,
and a cotton boss to grin.

And it takes workbreakingbacks
to make that paddle wheel spin.

THE STRANGEST CHRISTMAS TREE

I was barely a teenager
when I got my first camera.

My father surprised me
for my 14th birthday,
and I couldn't stop
taking pictures to lift me up
all that dreary November.

But it was just before Christmas
that I snapped my best shot.

It was outside a shotgun shack
near Midnight, not the time of day,
but the name of a town near mine.

I'd heard about
this colorful fortune teller
everybody said was kind.

I'd heard her warmth
was famous for
lighting up the dark days
of the Midnight poor.

She was quite a character,
and we hit it off when we met
in the yard outside her shack...

She was cautious at first,
especially cause I was
a white girl with a camera,
but she opened up in time.

She trusted me enough
to explain how
all the milk bottles
got on the scraggly tree
in her back yard.

It had to do with how
she sobered up her husband.

She was crazy for blues players,
but she had been afraid
to marry one, cause she believed
playing the Devil's music
always led to a short life
and an eternity in Hell.

But she married her
guitar-playing husband anyway,
cause she saw he had
the longest lifelines
in any palm she ever read.

One day he told her in tears
how he'd learned play.

He'd learned from an older man
who'd snap his fingers
with a switch every time
he made a mistake,
and sometimes when he didn't.

To forget the small-boy sting,
he needed a lot of booze
when he avoided picking up
his guitar, and a lot more
when he didn't.

To help out her hurting man,
she convinced him
she could trap his sting
in a milk bottle.

Somehow he believed her,
though it took
at least twenty bottles
to capture his stinging pain.

She put them on the branches
of the scraggly tree
to remind them both
a cure was possible.

She actually got him sober,
and he played a lot better.

He now could play
the devil's music free of fear,

cause they both believed
the bottles were an amulet
against the eternal sting
of the Devil.

# # #

I was happy that year
and glad to be alive,
glad to make new friends,
glad to hear non-stinging blues,
glad to take my best pictures
at Midnight,
glad to capture the strangest
and most touching Christmas tree
I ever saw the whole rest
of my midnight life
on my glad teenager film.

CHARITABLE LETTERS

I can feel a restless wigglin'
in a place I just don't itch.
I can feel some good news comin'
when my kneebone feels a twitch.

So, write me a lovin' letter,
mail it in the lonesome air.
Stuff it full of mercy,
it's sore needed everywhere.

I can feel some kindness comin'
in my torn and worn-out arm.
I can feel some mercy shinin'
in the shadows of my palm.

So, mail me some lovin' lines
I can hold in my sharecropper hand.
We need more mercy in the shadows
of this sinking bottom land.

'BOUT TAKEN ALL I CAN

On a Monday, bought me a sofa.
On a Tuesday, my rider was impressed.
On a Wednesday, we made that sofa wobble.
On a Thursday, it got repossessed.

Now, I just 'bout taken,
'bout taken all I can.
Ever was a devil without any horns,
certainly was that furniture man.

On a Monday, dreamt I was so lucky.
On a Tuesday, I had bananas for my meal.
On a Wednesday, bet all my lucky numbers.
On a Thursday, hit and run by that policy wheel.

Now, I just 'bout taken,
'bout taken all I can.
Ever was a devil without any hooves,
certainly was that policy man.

On a Monday, made up some hootch,
On a Tuesday, it went right to my head.
On a Wednesday, revenue man came calling.
On a Thursday, my butt was full of lead.

Now, I just 'bout taken,
'bout taken all I can.
Ever was a devil without any tail,
certainly was that revenue man.

On a Sunday, went to church.
On a Monday, the preacher came to call.
Next day, he stole my chicken,
Same day, he stole my gal.

Now that preacher sure has taken,
'bout taken all he could.
He gave that cackler to the Devil,
And my gal a-diddlin' in the woods.

THE INVENTOR OF THE GAS MASK

"George?"

"Yes, sir?"

"About that buffet flat..."

"Yes, sir."

"Write down the address,
will you, George?"

"Yes, sir."

As the train sped on,
George wrote down the address
of a club where black performers
put on enough obscene acts
to please a white businessman
with bulging pockets.

# # #

Never mind their real names,
all Pullman porters
were always called "George"
after the inventor
of the posh sleeping car,
George Pullman.

# # #

Yes, sir. Pullman porters
sure had it made.
Yes, sir, they did.
By waiting on the rich,
they could even travel
to places like Cleveland
and hear about great inventors
like Garrett Morgan.

Not many of their race
had that privilege.

Not many of the passengers
who slept on the white sheets
ever heard of Garrett Morgan.

No, sir.

You see, he was
the wrong color for inventors.

No, few comfortable sleepers,
tucked in their Pullman berths,
knew his name.

Not now.

Not now that the Great War
was long forgotten,
and the armistice too,
for those in peaceful berths.

# # #

endless places whizzing by
endless blues staying right here
blurs in the night
blues all the time
shoes to shine blur
blues still scuffed blur
blur blur blur
night blueses into blue night
cleave land.

Off duty in Cleveland,
the porters stopped calling
each other George
for, off the train, they weren't
"George's boys" any more.

In a local juke joint
at the wrong end of town,
they were talking
about Garrett Morgan.

They knew all too well
white troops in the trenches
of the Great War
knew his name for certain.

The troops had heard
the gas mask was invented
by a black man,
so they refused to wear one—
till the mustard gas
was thicker than their prejudice.

# # #

The off-duty porters both laughed
when they found out each had
the same dream.

It was to wear a gas mask
every time they had to fluff up
another rich man's pillow.

ALL OF THE ANGLES ARE SLIGHTLY OFF

On the whitelined streets
of the small cotton town,
all the building lines
are slightly off.

Each one has its own bias.

It is the night before Christmas,
not December 24th,
but a Saturday night
in the broiling summer,
the one free day
in the black work week.

The night before the one free day,
the fat man with the beard
carries no sack of gifts,
but continually shakes hands
with the fat end of an inherited whip.

And parables asking for mercy
in the remembrance of
somebody's birthday
might just as well be
in Aramaic.

"*If* today was Christmas Eve,
and *if* tomorrow was Christmas day,"
sings a tired bluesman...

But today isn't,
and tomorrow isn't either.

Not in this town
where all of the angles
are slightly off.

GOT UP ALL QUIET

I thought of telling my man
it can't go on this way.

But he was fast asleep
and snoring like a hound dog.

I thought of telling him
I was tired of being
a hound dog's woman.

He snored on,
like he was gnawing
on a fat dream bone.

So, in the morning,
I got up all quiet
and stayed that way
all day.

DOGS STALKING CATS

And, I so tired of all these dogs
stalking cats in every rain.
And I'm so tired of seeing rainbows
ending up inside a drain.

And I'm so tired of hoeing dirt
and seeing devils in the deep.
And I'm so tired-tired-tired
of no relief from sleep.

Cause nothing's gonna change
come beating rain or beating sun.
You just wake up every day
'specting half and getting none.

AIN'T NO ONE HERE

You gotta plant
some measly garden,
you gotta plant it
all by yourself.
Ain't no one here
gonna plant it for you,
you got to plant it
all by yourself.

You gotta pull up
a bucket of sadness,
you gotta pull it up
all by yourself.
Ain't no one here
gonna pull it up for you,
you gotta pull it up
from inside yourself.

You gotta steal away
in that dark, dank alley.
You gotta steal away
all by yourself.
Ain't no one here
gonna steal away for you,
you gotta steal
time for yourself.

And you gotta get laid
in some lonesome graveyard,
you gotta get laid there
all by yourself.
Ain't no one here
gonna lay there for you
you gotta lay unmarked
all by yourself.

PART THREE: THE LONE CAT SURVIVES

AT THE END OF THE MISSISSIPPI

At the end of the Mississippi,
the richest fertile soil.

At the end of the Mississippi,
the Empire of King Cotton.

At the end of the Mississippi,
lots of farmers in debt,
bleeding from the ploughshares
of sharecropping.

At the end of the Mississippi,
a new form of slavery
with no angry Abolitionist to care.

At the end of the Mississippi,
a spiffy Klansman in a three piece suit.

At the end of the Mississippi,
the richest crop of Delta Blues

At the end of the Mississippi,
a down-heels farmer dreaming of Chicago,
electricity, and a store-made guitar.

At the end of the Mississippi,
Muddy Waters dreaming
of a way out at the other end
of the Mississippi.

NEW RABBIT ALLEY BLUES

(for Rabbit Brown)

Times ain't now
nothin' like they used to be
used to bunnyhop in the alley,
now I'm on my knees.

And if you don't want me,
why doncha tell me so?
Don't hang me on your line
like you do all your clothes.

Cause I been lookin' for sugar,
and here you give me salt.
If you gonna pepper my tail,
don't ask me to somersault.

Hey, one day a week,
it's hallelujah from the pews.
Other six, you're on your knees
chasing the Rabbit Alley blues.

Done seen better days,
but I'm puttin' up with these.
Done seen better dogs—
that's the blues of every flea.

SINGING FURNITURE

THE TIME:

The late thirties, when white record producers could make a handsome profit by recording black bluesmen. They would transport them up north to record in the back of furniture stores. It was the time when you gave the bluesman $5 and half a bottle of hootch, and you brought in hundreds, if you were a furniture store owner with initiative.

THE PLACE:

Al's Furniture on Beale Street in Memphis.

THE PLAYERS:

Al of Al's Furniture
Martha, his angry wife
Clem, a close friend of Martha's
Tangle-Eye, a blues singer from Mississippi

THE PLOT:

Martha is talking to Clem.

"He got me into all this
because we started stocking
phonograph cabinets.
Al never got over the idea
of hearing his furniture *sing,*
as he put it...

We then started stocking all kinds
of phonograph records
to go with the singing furniture."

"How much are the records?"

"75 cents each."

"That much?"

"Sure enough. We can get it.
Customers come in here
every payday like clockwork.
At first, that was OK with me.
We was raking it in like this..."

Here Martha puts her right hand
over her left fist.

"Noticed you got a brand new dress
out of it. Nice one too.
Nice and tight."

"Yep. But can you believe it?
He goes all the way to Mississippi
to bring this guy Tangle-Eye
up here to Beale Street.
What a broken-toothed country bumpkin.
I'll tangle his eye, believe you me.
Guys like that toast my grits.
And all Al does is this..."

Here Martha rubs her thumb
against her first two fingers.

Tangle-Eye's voice comes from the back room:

A married man's a fool
to think that his wife
don't love nobody else but him.
She'll stick by you
your whole friggin' life
although chances is mighty slim...

Martha jerks her thumb
toward the back room.

"He's back there all the time
fiddlin' and jerkin' them dials all around
this-a-way and that-a-way
like he was married to them.
And he don't have clue one
how his wife really feels..."

"You doing anything later?"

"Nah. He's taking Tangle-Eye
back to Indianola tonight.
My back door latch'll be open
as usual.

But wait, I forgot... Tonight, Sweet Cakes,
you can come in the front... "

TOBY PITCHMAN BLUES

When the blues pick up your scent,
don't know where your luck all went,
buy a TOBY, it'll bring it all home...
When your fingers gettin' all bony,
and you hate waking up lonely,
buy a TOBY and you'll never sleep alone...
Now, just stroll on up,
put your last dollar down,
take home a lucky TOBY,
and get ready to get on down.
You know that special rider?
You'll be snugglin' right beside her,
if you step up and take this TOBY home.

When the cat got your pajamas,
and you're walkin' on skinned bananas,
just a buck to bring your luck on home...
Say bad luck done swiped your pride,
and you got no blind to ride,
Toby'll take away your lonesome moan...
Now, you wanna get to heaven,
and you got no time to pray,
just buy yourself this TOBY,
you'll be flying all the way.
Why stay double-crossed in Hell,
with no soul left to sell?
Just a buck to bring your luck back home...

Say your engine lost its throttle,
you're as empty as a drunk's bottle,
buy a TOBY and get yourself on home...
Don't be a motherless son,
this here TOBY is the one,
just the thing to bring your luck home...
*Don't steal no rabbit's foot,
give the black cat back his bone.
The genie in the bottle
just bought a TOBY of his own.*
Step on up and don't be sore,
discount on ten or more,
just a buck to throw your dogged luck a bone.

COOLIN' BOARD

And it's all over weepin' and wailin',
the Depression was creepin' coast to coast,
when I got hit upside by that letter
sayin' she done give up the ghost.

So, I caught the next thing a-smoking,
doncha know it was that Yeller Dog Road?
When I made it back down to the bottom,
she was stretched out on the coolin' board.

Well, her mother wouldn't say howdy,
and her father sure told me goodbye.
Couldn't look at any of the family,
they all just give me the evil eye...

Now, I was holdin' back all the tears
till that leavin' sun went down,
couldn't find nobody in the bottom
to throw my lovin' arms around.

Couldn't tell how far I was fallin',
I was sinkin' for all I was worth.
Seems like I was deep in the ocean
in the driest place on the earth.

Don't miss your sweet well water
till tears run your insides dry.
Don't miss your sweet high yeller
till there's old pennies on her eyes...

PLAYED HIM 'GAINST THE ACE

Well, I played him 'gainst the King,
and it made the dealer sing.
And I played him 'gainst the ace,
it was a starvation in my face,
that Jack o' Diamonds
was a hard card to play.

And I was on that Delta Queen,
tryin' to turn my money green.
And I was on that dammed show boat,
kept my pants, but lost my coat,
That Jack o' Clubs
was a hard card to play...

Miss Luck was right there sayin' *My, My,*
all the time I was ridin' high.
But the Jack bird-dogged me again,
stole her when I lost the game.
That Jack o' Hearts
was a hard card to play.

Now I'm a total wreck
hit by every card in the deck.
And I'm as shuffled as I can be,
cause the deck keeps shufflin' me.
That Jack o' Spades was a bitchin' card to play.

Cards'll rob you
when you got a full cup.
When you're going down,
cards don't hold you up.
Even Jokers ain't no funny cards to play...

RESONATIN' THE DOZENS

=1=
I was born in the 12th month,
spent twelve nights playin' blues on Mars
and I got twelve stars in my pockets
playing resonator guitars.

=2=
Well, folks round here don't want
that smokin' stuff you sell.
They tell me God don't like ugly,
say, boy, your home's in Hell.

=3=

Yeah? Well, I can see your bulgin' eyes
way too big for your little lids.
Too bad your father and mother
didn't have them no damn kids.

=4=

Yeah? Your mamma was a taddy,
and your daddy was a pole.
You got frog ways in your innards
and you're gonna croak on jelly roll.

=5=

Yeah, if I was a flippin' frog,
I'd sure be satisfied.
All day long, I'd sure be flippin'
my tongue in your flippin' eye.

=6=

You're dumb as a pounded thumb,
and your head is so damn thick.
You look like some frog beat you
with an ugly stick.

=7=

Hey, you better watch it,
callin' ugly all you see.
My mama didn't pull up no sheet
so sleep could creep up on me.

=8=

Yeah? I'm gonna knock your door ajar,
and make your jelly into jam.
That bullfrog stuff you been shootin'
ain't worth a jumpin' damn.

=9=
If you keep breakin' all this wind,
I'm gonna break your jaw.
Tell my daddy down in Hell
it got broke by his son-in-law.

=10=
Well, you ain't no Devil's son-in-law
and he don't catch you when you fall.
When you married Satan's daughter,
she sure starched your overalls.

=11=
I'm gettin' flippin' tired
of all your flippin' drool.
I ain't gonna resonate no dozens
with such a flippin' fool.

=12=
You think you're tough as Stagolee,
but you ain't all that mean.
Cause I'm the luckiest rounder
ever counted past thirteen...

PENCIL FOR A CAPO

Abraham was poor.

So poor he couldn't afford
a capo for his guitar,
so he had to use
a pencil and a rubber band.

So poor that, even though
he was named for a President,
he's never seen a white rose garden.

He's always, always in debt,
though he works hard from *can't to can't,*
that is, from when he can't
see the daybreak sun
till when he can't
see it after dark.

While it's up, the sun
fries him like the gutted chicken
at a Klan barbecue.

On Sunday, he gives a few pennies
to the collection plate,
but the church service
does nothing for him anymore,
because he suspects the church
holds out hope of a sunny heaven
only to make him work harder.

He does still worship
something on Sunday though:
his scarred guitar.

But, just now, as he was
stealing a few moments
playing it, the rubber band
snapped and sent his poor pencil
across the room...

There it broke the glass
in the only frame he had, the one he'd
saved up more than a year for,
the one which held his only picture
of Abraham Lincoln.

THREE PHOTOS OF SLEEPY SLIM

My first photograph showed Sleepy Slim, the bluesman from the Beale Street Jug Band, slumping over his guitar. It has an extra sound hole, made by his fierce attack on its flat top. The Beale Street Jug Band was really famous in its day, but now Slim, the lead guitarist, is all but forgotten. He's run out of small change, and has to use a broom wire for the first string. His pained expression in the photo shows he thinks it sounds awful. The days when he put down sounds like liquid silver on his new guitar are long gone. His day in the sun only lasted as long as the twilight.

Wind my motor, mama,
till I got a wound-up spring,
Put that needle in that hole,
and play that Beale Street Swing...

Double entendres don't mean much anymore, now that his turn table and life are all broken down. I feel his pain so much, my own heart loses its spring. I give him fifty bucks for letting me take the photo. His head lifts. Twilight still has a little more light...

In the second photo, I caught him at dinner, eating a plate of fat back and pinto beans. He tells me the rats in his kitchen were extra mean this year. They got the pork chop and left him the pintos. In the photo, his eyes are almost completely covered by fallen lids.

You don't believe I love you,
just look at the fool I been.
You don't believe I'm sinking,
look at the hole I'm in...

In the third photo he let me take, for my book on what happened to the old bluesmen, Sleepy Slim is sitting on the battered mattress of his Murphy bed. He can barely keep it from folding back up into the wall. He's showing me an old dummy he used to use in his medicine show act. The dummy sits up tall and its bright painted bulging eyes see nothing. His lips don't move. Sleepy Slim's barely do either. But not because he can no longer throw his voice. *I got nothing to say no more, this here dummy's talking for me, and he ain't sayin' nothing.* I doubt Sleepy Slim cares if a picture is worth a thousand words. I feel about a thousand-and-one short myself.

THE LONE CAT SURVIVES

The Lone Cat Survives.
When he was just eight,
his step-father put him in a burlap bag,
hung the bag from a tree,
and used it for a punching bag.
The Lone Cat survived.

The Lone Cat survives.
He played the twelve string
like it had twenty-four strings.
He once met Leadbelly,
and Leadbelly put him down...

There was only one
King of the Twelve String,
and he treated the Lone Cat
like some lone pawn in a pawn shop.
The Lone Cat survived.

The Lone Cat survives.
In the sixties, white producers
discovered him, though
he was never lost.
He made a couple of records.
They didn't sell,
not like Leadbelly's.
His label dropped him.
The Lone Cat survived.

The Lone Cat survives.
The records were re-issued
after he died.
On one he says:
*I'm gonna do something
you don't always hear
on a record.*
Then he dances a Buck and Wing,
while he plays twelve string
at the same time...

The Lone Cat's CD is alive with joy,
alive with vibrant dancing, singing, playing,
as if he had more
than twenty-four heartstrings.

The Lone Cat still survives.

PART FOUR: MERCY LANE

BLUES IN YOUR EAR

It's like when you get
water in your ear.

Sometimes it helps
to get it out
if you hop around
a lot.

# # #

There's no remedy
like that
for the blues.

Once they get
into your ear,
they stay there.

Although sometimes
it's quite natural
to hop around a lot
when you hear them.

SIDETRACK

Let me be your sidetrack
till your main line come.
I'm do more switching mama
than your mainline ever done.

She put that hot-foot powder
all around that boxcar door.
That rider kokomo-ed me
way down in Arkansas.

Spoken:
Way down, yeah, I'm tellin' you,
way down rollin', way down rockin',
way down in Arkan-rollin'-saw.
You rounders know what I mean.
Over the hills and way down underneath,
that's what I'm talkin' bout.

I'll be your sidetrack, mama,
and we'll roll that highball too.
Don't mind lowballin' none,
long as I'm doin' it with you.

So, I want you to rock me, baby,
till that ghost train cries "boo-hoo."
Want you to reel to that rockin'
till the cowcatcher cries "mooo."

THE FORCE FIELD OF SON HOUSE

In the Gaslight Cafe
on MacDougal Street
in Greenwich Village,
Son House sang
some of the pictures
off the wall.

Impressionist prints
started experiencing
post impressions.

In the publicity stills,
several urban singer-songwriters
felt their photographed eyes
come to life.

Long lost, the force field
of Son's Delta voice
set New York City music
in new directions.

And, as he sang deep blues
in the Village cafe,
the stale, still coffee
was percolating again,
and the tired pastries hopped,
as if fresh from the oven.

DREAMING OF THE IMMENSITY

He came to talk at City College all about the field trips he'd taken
south in search of the real country rural acoustic blues and it was a
killer I'm telling you cause he was so full of the blues lifeforce and
blues phrases like *bury my body down by the highway side so my ol'
evil spirit can catch a Greyhound bus and ride* and *I asked her how
bout it and she said all right but she never showed up at my cabin last
night* and Gullah English who ever heard of it flowing like serpentine
river of language and phrases rusty for crab doing the buzzard lope on
Georgia islands time forgot and bones clicking and hambones slapping
thighs and chests in the brickyard and Maxfield Parrish's wife was
down there too songcatching and the guy who was saying all this was
married to a magic woman who was writing a life of Kerouac and I saw
in the college lecture hall a forty-foot scroll unrolling and there was a
gang of jazz blues written on that too and like Ezekiel I wanted to eat
it up so it was inside my innards and whetted my appetite and dry
bones and now heard the word of the blues calling in the wilderness of
cotton and I wanted to hit the dusty roads with him and I wanted so
to ride the railroad earth with him and leave No-no-no November
behind and please if I only had a wife like her and a life like his and I
was dreaming in the immensity of it all all the while he talked and my
mind was all wandering like all the wild geese in the west and I wanted
to fly south in the summer and it took all the blue diamond courage I
had to ask him please could I come along on the next songcatching trip
and they must be singing the blues right now in the land where the
best crop is the blues and please please take me along on that sliding
Delta highway 51 or 61 running right by the door to what I loved so
much and who wanted to keep reading Anglo-Saxon riddles about
seafarers when you could ride the flood waters of America and please
pretty please with sweet potato pie on top don't shoo me away like
some fly please notice what you liberated in my jailhouse head take me

with you when you go doncha leave me here with a long chain on and so please hear my pleas but when I went up to the podium he responded with oh-so so so very politely just one word:

"No."

SINGULAR STING

even when sung
with a buzzing voice
by a Texas girl misfit
all strung out on nectar
and Southern comfort
in her thin-veins

even when buzzed
by honeyed hair kids
following puberty's dance
away from their parents'
rigid combs

even when doo-whopped
at the buzzing Apollo
by black- and yellow-gowned dolls
with hair done up
like bee hives

even though plural when sung,
the blues stay singular
whenever they sting

DREAM HEART DRUNK ON BLUES

Last night I dreamt I drank some blues
and my heart danced all out of control.
It was filled to the brim with spirituals
poured over rocks of rattle and roll.

Went to bed sober as that judge
who'd paid all his chain gang dues.
My dream heart was dancing on his bench
barrel-housing the Not-Guilty blues.

It jumped the freight train of the moon,
rode midnight tracks to a jook-joint Mars.
There were bluesman from the Speak Easy Way
with comets shooting from their glowing guitars.

And, when it's snooze alarm time on Judgment Day,
and when the good news says bad news is done,
Devil's Food Blues and Angel Cake Spirituals
will dance way past Kingdom Come.

BAFFLED

The clues were all there,
but the solution to the crime
wasn't.

There was that bloody noose
at the end of that blue-twisted
rope.

There was that blue-blooded stain
on the white sheets sent
to the Chinese
laundry.

There was that black record
of a blues singer's moan
bearing such deep
and hurtful blue
scratches.

The clues to a continuous crime
baffled the wits of Charlie Chan.

The same way they baffle
the compassion of anyone
investigating the blues.

MARRIED IN MEMPHIS

W.C. Handy dozes while waiting
for a train to take him home
to Memphis.

Something ancient and mythic
happens in that echoing train station,
something that brings W.C.
home before he got there,
something that resonates
in the soft switch yard, where
the lines of his veins
cross the arteries of his heart.

It's a guitar with wake-up strings
being played by a ragged bluesman
with a jagged bottle
on the third finger
of his left hand.

That broken bottle neck
goes straight to W.C.'s heart,
and that very day,
Handy marries the blues.

He boards the train
and brings his bride
with him back to Beale Street.

They live not necessarily happily
ever after, but there is never
any question of a divorce.

MERCY LANE

Many bluesmen were born blind,
in the dark physically, but never in spirit.
Blues and gospel don't see alike?
not quite 20/20, but pretty damn near it.

Cause the blues possess a saving grace,
you stay blind, but still you see.
The blues possess enough amazement
to save the wretched like you and me.

For the blues outlast faith healing,
and the faith healer's rods and cones.
The blues see into the feeling heart,
and light up the parts unknown.

The blues are a rod and cone miracle.
They are better than any white cane.
The blues have no need of dark glasses
when they walk down Mercy Lane.

BLUES LIKE THE TIDES

Blues like the tides
come and grow.
Sometimes you're full,
sometimes you're low.
Sometimes the driftwood
is all you know.
Blues stain the heart
with their tidal flow.

Blues lower the heart
at every tide.
Blues pull like moons
on the sea inside.
Blues seep right through
any toughened hide.
Blues are the undertow
to your inner sides.

Blues come like floods
to any levied greed.
When we feel want,
they put us in need.
When blues want surrender,
we must concede.
When we can't follow,
blues take the lead.

CHAPTER TWO

BLUES ARCHAEOLOGISTS

PART ONE: FRAGMENTS PIECED TOGETHER

THE BLUES ARCHAEOLOGIST

Fragments of the blues
of the late 20's
pieced together:
it was one way
to learn to write.

As when Leadbelly said:
I didn't make this one,
I just fixed it.

Fixing together found fragments:
the archaeology of the blues.

Finding the matched edges
of disparate shards:
the archaeology of the blues
of a rich unearthed
and surprising civilization.

# # #

From one source, he already had:
Ever dream lucky,
wake up cold in hand.
and from another:
Ever look through muddy waters
till you see dry land.

Sure enough,
when he put them together,
the edges matched.

# # #

As in all old blues,
the organizing principle
was not a narrative,
but the linkage
between emotional states.

The blues didn't tell a story
so much as they
told the feelings
connected to the story.

The blues singer saw
similarities between
two or more psychological states
and united them,
as an archaeologist would
material fragments.

# # #

The tune was pieced together too,
a riff from an old song
juxtaposed with another,
till the fragments of both
noted themselves together.

Both lyrics and tunes
were playful montages...

The blues archaeologist
put two tunes together,
and created an original verse:

*Believe I'll rag my broom,
believe I'll dust my mop:
this riff is so delicious,
I believe I'll lick my chops...*

# # #

The blues archaeologist
had a thought:
*If you want to know
how to fit together
the dug-up fragments
left behind by
the blues civilization,
keep digging deeper.*

BIGGER THAN THE LOUISIANA TERRITORY

Thomas Jefferson purposefully
left off a reference to the fact
that he had been President
on the monument he designed
for his own grave.

He listed only three
living achievements,
and being President
wasn't one of them.

Everything was left off
the gravestone
of Blind Lemon Jefferson.

That is, if there had been
a gravestone.

His gravestone
turned out to be
nothing but thin air.

No living achievements
could be listed,
but that was hardly
Blind Lemon's wish.

One of his best-known lyrics
asked poignantly:
There's one kind favor I ask of you:
please see that my grave is kept clean.

Considering you can't even find it,
his grave turned out to be
a cruel symbol:

One kind favor?

Sorry, Lemon,
posterity grants you
no favor and even less kindness...

#

An old blues lyric goes:
*Blues jumped a rabbit,
and ran him a country mile...*

Blues jumped the Third President,
and ran him a whole country's mile.

Blues jumped Blind Lemon,
and ran him all the way
to an unmarked American grave.

Blues jumped the country
and ran it all the way
to the heart of melancholy.

Both Jeffersons knew
that heart was bigger
than the whole
Louisiana Territory.

THE AFTERSHOCK

Brief Biographical Note on Nora Nolan Hurd (1900-1964)

A major figure of the Harlem Renaissance, Nora Nolan Hurd was all but forgotten in her later years. She died in poverty in a state-run Florida nursing home. None of the residents and none of the attendants knew anything about her extensive writings.

Nora wrote in just about every form known to those who must write or die: poems, short stories, novels, plays, essays, songs, folkloric studies, and a screenplay. Her intense anger at prejudice is present in everything she wrote. There were countless examples of this in her own experience, but one will suffice to make her point. During a visit to the doctor, she was once asked to wait in the closet instead of in the waiting room. Very sensitive, almost too sensitive to live, she was devastated by such condescension. She was hospitalized six times for depression and suicidal ideation. As was mentioned above, she died poor and ignored. She might as well have expired in a closet.

Modern critics have done much to revive her reputation. Though the manuscripts she had in her possession were lost at her death, some of her journals have survived. The following entry, written in 1922, was not published until 20 years after her death.

January 12, 1922

Dear Journal,

It's in the cards. I can't believe I actually got the sweet grant from that flourpasty woman whose remedy for pale boredom is her Tarot deck. That, and a carved mask, not from her ancestral homeland, but from mine.

The cards and the mask spoke to her, and boy did they yell out good news. She's agreed to bankroll a field trip for me. I'm going south to be a folklorist, to lure the folk into telling me rainbow stories, and to wear the coat of a songcatcher of many colors. It's a golden opportunity to smash all the cruel cliches about Uncle Tom Remus. The Noble Savage gets bankrolled to come back and tell The Bankroller that my Aunt Jemima ain't no more real than her Uncle Sam...

Maybe the flourpasties should establish the Nobel Savage Award, and catch the next thing a-smokin' all the way to Stockholm, so they can watch a Minstrel Show as their white gloves hold clouded opera glasses. If I won the prize, I'd blow up the dumb white dam which holds back the singing black river. After all, Journal, can there be a more appropriate aftershock for the white man who invented dynamite?

EAST RIVER LOVE

If you're lovin' somebody and they ain't lovin' you,
that's love you might as well throw in the East River.
--Leadbelly

Is there unrequited love
for the blues?

East River love
for the blues?

If you're lovin' them,
and they ain't...

But wait.

If you're lovin' them,
the blues'll always
give you back more lovin'
than anybody
has ever thrown
into a New York City river.

FLYING OVER FOREIGN LANDS

Just a near-sighted blues singer,
can't see any better than I play.
People say I should not sing these eyeglass blues,
I'm up here singing them anyway.

And when I pick up this scarred flattop,
I believe I lay it on the line.
Everybody's got a way of surviving,
I believe I'm up here singing mine.

Just a mild-mannered blues reporter,
I avoid those phone booths when I can.
Blues travel faster than a speeding bullet,
they outfly even Superman.

And without moving a muscle,
I'm flying over foreign lands.
And I got all the pain of the darkening Delta
right here in the palm of my hand.

Just a near-sighted blues singer,
can't see any better than I play.
And if guitar playing were declared illegal,
you know I just could not stay away...

PART TWO: WHITE FLAG

RAGGED WHITE FLAG

I give up, I sure enough surrender:
my life's one big fender-bender.
I got the message, and it's not good news,
so I'm waving these white flag blues.

I'm deflated, I'm checkmated
I'm dissipated, I'm alligatored.
No slippery slope, but a sticky drag
wagging that old and ragged white flag.

So, I'm crying *Great, Great Uncle*,
guess I'm just a Shakespearean nuncle.
My hopes fell with the low tide,
and my white flag's up there on high.

My whole fiery family's takin' turns,
Nephew Flame, Niece Singe, and Uncle Burns,
all singing on the sinking stern,
Just name all your surrender terms.

So, I'm reasoning with no rhyme,
and I'm as talkative as some mime.
My white flag ain't worth a dime,
and it's more ragged all the time.

BLUES FOR THE FLAGLESS

Praha. Today the locally-known blues singer, cubist painter, novelist, and inventor, Marek Mikusek died of a heart attack while singing to a small audience of admirers. He was 55, but many of his friends described him as ageless.

He is best remembered for his invention of the 9-string resonator guitar. A fine blues musician, he also composed many humorous blues such as *Ten Gallon Czech, Rio Vltava,* and *Blues for the Flagless.*

Mikusek was an active participant in the community known as "Czexans," that is, people of Czech heritage who now live in Praha, Texas. He moved to Texas from Prague in 1912. His song, *Year of the Titanic,* chronicles his early experiences in America. The song is full of irony. Having escaped from the militaristic repression of the Austro-Hungarian Empire, he was retained in a prison camp in Dallas during the War-to-End-All-Wars. He was a firm conscientious objector, though he was classed by the military as a suspicious alien. He never got over this Kafkaesque experience. Though known locally as heavy drinker, he always said he drank more from "the well of American sadness" than he ever did from a bottle.

Mikusek also painted in a cubist style. He tried several times to have galleries display his art, but was always turned down because his painting style was "too foreign to appeal to American buyers." His reaction was not surprising; he said he had been "labeled a suspicious alien once again."

He also authored a strange novel, which he self-published. The story is set inside a guitar, and all of the characters are musical notes, "some whole, some half, some quarter." Some of the quarter-notes, who are called "Flagwavers," want the guitar to play sentimental patriotic songs. Others, the whole notes, called "Flagless," want blues and jazz. The author is obviously on the side of the latter.

The funeral is scheduled for Monday the 12th at 4PM. It will be held in the small church of St. Wit here in Praha. Mikusek never married, and is survived only by his novel, his paintings, his songs, and his unique 9-string resonator guitar, which contained for him a whole world of "Blues for the Flagless."

BREAKING UP JUST BEFORE DAYBREAK

Laid up, and sick on a broken bed,
face turned toward the peeling wall... *(twice)*
Thought I could hear the sweetest sound,
like my good gal when she call...

All night just rollin' and tumblin'
I heard her sweet voice call my name... *(twice)*
Talking bout when times were different
and we both saw things the same.

Thinkin' bout those sweet good times
fore everything just fell apart... *(twice)*
Thinkin' bout how lonesome you can get
when pains scurry cross your heart.

All night rollin' and a-tumblin'
while the blues grabbed all my dreams ...*(twice)*
Just me and my old ratty mattress,
both comin' apart at all the seams.

Breakin' up just before daybreak,
blues crawling all in my yard... *(twice)*
Must be love gnawin' at my heart,
a bedbug can't chew that hard...

ON TAPE

A rich man videotapes his possessions.
Insurance and silver have fine designs.
A poor man needs no vault for his song.
His real assurance is between its lines.

If you don't have a gleaming existence,
and no gloss to your untanned hide,
and nothing to put on video insurance,
your vault stays open, inside.

I'm not here to make a commercial,
personal best is all that I need.
I'm not after an instant replay,
but the right emotional speed.

This song won't make the pop charts.
It's not riches it's trying to create.
The freedom from taped possessions
is all I can put on tape.

SO EASY WHEN YOU KNOW HOW

We like to wobble,
but my Rider got bored,
so now we do it
on the running board...

And it's so easy,
yeah, I got it now.
This wobblin's easy
if you just know how.

I went to the barrelhouse,
and I had a few,
I lost my pants,
Rider, what a view...

But it's so easy,
yeah I got it now.
This dancin' naked's easy,
if you just know how.

My car broke down.
Took the long way home.
Nobody stopped.
I walked that road alone.

And it's not easy,
I can't get it, no-how.
This walkin' alone'd be easy,
if I'd only learn how...

Blues Like The Tides

PART THREE: MINUS TWO BLUES

ON THE LAM

I'm on the lam, I am, I am.
Aunt Jemima has lost her jam.
And we've lost the niece of Uncle Sam,
out in America, on the lam.

"Can't find the missing person report,"
that's all the snooping cop wrote.
I'm out there missing on the lam,
casting *HOPE* as my write-in vote.

Repeat chorus

He gave an arm and a leg too
fighting for us in Viet Nam.
Now he's homeless in his own hometown
spending Easter on the lam.

Repeat chorus

The Great Society was flowing,
but now it's trickled down.
It's not all that great when you're sleeping
on a grate in your hometown...

Repeat chorus

Mark Twain discovered a little too late
you can be witty and still be scammed.
King Arthur's table turns itself around
for a Connecticut Yank out on the lam.

Repeat chorus

"Bait and switch" is all you hear
in the shopping malls of the damned.
There're a lot more prisoners inside the mall
than the ones out on the lam.

CANDLE WICK

Used to feel like a candle wick,
burnt out at the core... *(twice)*
Used to feel like melted wax
all puddled on the floor.

This goddamned self-pity,
why do I love it so? *(twice)*
I got to throw away my snuffer
and remember when I glowed.

So, when I see some rising smoke,
I'll remember the candle's flame... *(twice)*
And when I'm all burnt out, I'll know
there's a chance for light again...

THREE TIMES TWENTY

My bells are sounding a little more cracked,
but one thing rings clear and true... *(twice)*
I'm way over three times twenty,
and I know just what I have to do...

I've got to find new ways to freedom
before I'll get my will... *(twice)*
I've got to drink up my full portion
before death wipes up the spills.

I've got to eat delicious blues
before I meet their baker... *(twice)*
I've got to shake hands with an underdog,
and shake paws with the undertaker.

Got six years on my old friend Sixty,
four less on my new friend Seventy... *(twice)*
I'm happy to shake the hand of both
while my hand's this side of heavenly...

MINUS TWO BLUES

I'm motherless and fatherless,
sisterless and brotherless too.
My days are wheatless and meatless,
and my floursack's turned to glue.

A wallet soaked in spilled blues
and pocket coins with two sides dead.
Only two short of a two dollar bill,
and postage due on the stamp on my head.

And I'm lacing up an orphan coat,
and turning up the collars on my shoes.
2 cents short of a wooden nickel
and melted pennies for a fuse.

I got an I. O. U. from King Midas
and a rubber check in my piggy bank.
My Thanksgiving's all I hoped for,
except for the giving and the thanks.

But I'm not complaining—no,
I'm not painting my corner blue.
My bit part's still worth two bits,
even if my two cents is minus two.

TAKEN TO THE CLEANERS

Well, I'm about the cleanest guy
that you have ever seen.
My last nickel is so shiny
and my last dollar's bleached of all its green.
And I'm so full of sloshing suds,
I could be living in a washing machine,
cause I've been taken to the cleaners
when I was already clean.

Yeah, I've been taken to the cleaners,
all hung out, and all gleams.
I'm all washed up, and coming apart
at each and every seam.
So much of me has washed away,
I am the size of a pinto bean—
so, get me out of this hamper,
cause I'm already clean.

It's so cold in this turned off dryer,
and the spin cycle's spinning hot.
My dots are polkaing on the line
without a single spot.
My double breasted's been cut in half,
and a clean breast is all I got.
If I could only find that missing sock,
I'd know the where, the how, and the what...

Spoken:
But since I can't, I don't.

PART FOUR: THE CLAPTONIAN THEOREM

THE BLUES OF A MAN OVERSTATED

Just look how you turned my life all around.
See how you diminished my pain.
And just when I left inspiration behind,
see how you bring back my spirit again.

And it's turnaround, turnaround,
see how love turns all around.
Nothing like turnaround loving
to spin you out of the Lost and Found...

You give back my mind in thinking,
you give my kindness back in kind.
And when I'm giving up and sinking,
you throw out such loving lifelines.

Repeat Chorus

So, here's the gift of a man overstated
to a woman who brought inner calm.
I just love your spiritual fingers
and the lifelines they trace in my palms.

THE HISTORY OF THE BLUES IN SIX GUITARS

"Only breathing matters more."
--Tom Standage, *A History of the World in Six Glasses*

=1=
The Diddley Bow

In the beginning,
the diddley bow...
a one stringed hypotenuse
between the upright porch post
and the flat porch floor...
but a whole genesis
for the creation
of the blues...

=2=
The Cigar Box

A couple more strings
stretched over a cigar box,
and a sharecropper
had a whole crop
of untaxed blues...

=3=
The Pawn Shop Gitfiddle

Cheap pawnshop gitfiddles
left behind for a ticket...

Pick one up
and pick out a tune
of redeemed dreams...

=4=
The Singing Axe

"In life I was quiet," says the maple,
"but in death, I sing."

An ax produces an axe guitar,
a dead tree a living guitar.

There are as many
blues roots underground
as you hear reaching
for the sky.

=5=
The Metal Resonator

When metal resonators hit the streets
from the northern assembly lines,
a new kind of blues
started to assemble way down home.

Steel-drivin' on the steel guitar
lifted the heart of the gandy dancer...

National was the brand name,
and they played national blues,
even when confined
to a very small region.

=6=
The Last Word on the Wall

Graffiti reverence on Westminster wall:
a new bridge for London:
Eric Clapton is God.

The roots of down-home guitar
have become an electric divinity...

The Claptonian theorem
of the diddley bow triangle.

Clapton knows where that came from...

He does these blues
in remembrance of poor
resurrected fingers...

PUB SIGN BLUES

Three *CATS ON A HOLIDAY* told a joke,
as they drank up *THREE TUNS* on a dare.
Everybody after rolled with laughter,
except *THREE NUNS AND A HARE.*

THE SILENT WOMAN told it in signing slang,
and made *THE QUACKING DUCK* her livelong fan.
A turkey laughed his *TURK'S HEAD* off,
cause *THE FLYING DUTCHMAN* had to land...

THREE SQUIRRELS told it down at *THE NUTSHELL*
and made *THE ROYAL OAK* bend.
THE GRAY DONKEY gladly lent his ears
to the bonnie asses and *THE BARLEY MAN.*

THE BARKING DOG woofed it to *THE WILDMAN*
who always enjoyed a barked joke.
THE WOODEN INDIAN laughed his headdress off
when he saw *THE POOR MAN* come unbroke.

Seems lightning once hit a couple up
on *THE BAG O' NAILS* cathouse roof.
They hit the ground still locked together
and that's the effing truth.

A bloke came by and saw them
frozen right there on the ground.
He then shouted in the cathouse door,
"Hey, girls, your sign fell down."

Chapter Two

KING'S ENGLISH BLUES

*Excerpt from the liner notes
of an imaginary anthology
of British Interpreters of American Blues*

Side One, Track 19
This'll Bring You Back
by Ralph McTell

Ralph McTell offers this version of the Mississippi John Hurt song called *I'm Satisfied.* McTell here blends the John Hurt version nicely with another version of the song recorded by the Memphis Jug Band. Ralph is known for shaking up an audience with his mastery of blues which originated in the States. His performances include these blues always interspersed with his own self-penned songs, such as *Streets of London* and *Zimmerman Blues,* the latter about Bob Dylan, whose real name is Zimmerman. As McTell well knows, Dylan did his homework, and studied acoustic blues in depth before he picked up that electric guitar, the one which shocked folk-song enthusiasts at that notorious Newport Folk Festival.

Here, McTell has done as well as anyone at accomplishing the impossible, that is, making a John Hurt song his own. Hurt's style is so distinctive, you always hear the original in every copy. At least as far as guitar styles go. With lyrics, though, you can find some interesting variations. For instance, McTell sings:

*I'm satisfied, I'm satisfied,
with my long cold shakers by my side...*

After singing that line, Ralph adds, "Whatever that is..." Honesty. Don't know something, admit it. Nothing pretentious about McTell's blues...

So, since these are liner notes, and I too had to do my homework. I looked up *shaker* in the Oxford American Dictionary. I can tell you for certain John Hurt is not referring to a religious sect. But I still have no clue. Sorry, Ralph, I let you down. I should point out, though, an interesting fact. The next entry after our puzzling word was *Shakespeare.*

Someone once said, "I hate Shakespeare cause the plays are all full of cliches." If anyone ever tells you that about the blues, ask them if *they* know what *a long cold shaker* is.

POOR AS A BIRD

Oh, singing blues, I have no friend like you.
You bring back the spectrum when I'm jay-bird blue.
But there's no monetary value on making music of your days,
livin' poor as a bird who but gives his song away...

Sometimes I think I have exactly what I need.
Other times I think I'm only livin' on bird seed.
But when the blues overtake St. Francis, a sparrow sings them all away.
His eye is on the sparrow who but sends blues on their way.

Bridge:
Poor as a meadowlark at the break of day,
poor as a clipped-wing raven when walking like a jay...

Oh, the space between song and silence keeps on worrying me,
depression flies between those two, when you're seeking to be free.
But there's no monetary value on making music of your days,
livin' rich as a bird who freely gives his song away.

PART FIVE: DIGGING DOWN DEEPER

RIDDLE ME THE BLUES

Western wind blows blues riddles
as the small rain down can rain.
A forceful olden dire wind
blows blues my way again.

The blues are a-comin in,
and they're comin' in as a riddle:

Who am I when I strike
down a serf and no one seems to care,
when I search the wounds of a knight
who died in the arms of another's wife,
when I strike like a mace through a shield
useless to protect any one from my attacks,
when I win every joust,
and when I riddle you
with the rusted chain-mail of sadness?

The western wind blows a riddle,
and here come the small rain blues again...

THE NEWSPAPERS OF THEIR TIMES

"If I don't read, my soul be lost."
--Blind Willie Johnson

Digging down. Old ballads.

Digging down. The newspapers of their times.

Digging down. Old blues in the olden times.

Digging down. *The Blues Standard* in the old ballads.

"Matty Groves and Adulterous Lover Murdered"
headlines *The Ballad Times.*

"Lord Randall Poisoned"
Sing all about it.

"Youth Dies For Love of Barb'ry Allen"
headlines *The Blues Globe.*

"Knight Slain Under Shield as Three Ravens Watch"

"Sir Patrick Spens Lies Fifty Fathom Deep"

"Hind Horn Caught in Sex Scandal"

"Thomas Rhymer Gone Missing"

"Child Finds More Blues in More Ballads"
headlines *The Modern Times*

Digging down.

My morning blues—
they're so much older
than my morning news.

ANONYMOUS WAS A BLUES WOMAN

" *Wild woman don't worry,*
wild woman don't have no blues..."
--Ida Cox

They created so much
and they never got the credit.

Ever see that modern bumper sticker:
Ginger Rogers did everything Fred Astaire did,
but backwards and on high heels.

How many dances have come down
from unknown women dancers
who never made it to bumper sticker fame?

There are blues,
and there are blues,
but the worst are those
you have to suffer anonymously.

THE BROKEN OCEAN FLOOR

"When he heard about that mighty shock,
oughta seen him do the Eagle Rock..."
--Leadbelly describing Jack Johnson's
reaction to his denial of passage
on *The Titanic*

Didn't God move on the water?
sings the Georgia Sea Islander
about April the 14th day,
the cruelest day for *The Titanic.*

Artifacts of the famous wreck
are like sirens singing
to an iceberg who has no feeling
for the broken ocean floor.

Of course, the Sea Islander
knows God moves *under* the ocean too.

So many human blues lie there,
no longer on the deck
of what the Sea Islander saw
as a floating Tower of Babel.

RESURFACING IN APPALACHIA

Look in the American mountains
for the English old ballad blues.

You can find such old song artifacts
buried deep in Appalachian soil.

Dig down further.

Songcathers do best
when they listen to voices
who sing of the old-time blues
way, way, way
under the ground
where they,
and they, and they
find their roots.

Blues Like The Tides

CHAPTER THREE

THIRTEEN LUCKY POETS

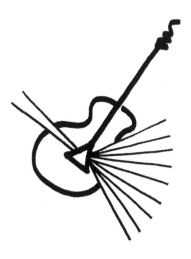

INTRODUCTION: VOICES AND VISIONS

Chapter Three is based on the series shown on the Public Broadcasting System in 1988. The series was called *Voices and Visions*. It presented one hour programs on each of the following poets:

(1)   Walt Whitman
(2)   Emily Dickinson
(3)   Robert Frost
(4)   Wallace Stevens
(5)   William Carlos Williams
(6)   Ezra Pound
(7)   Marianne Moore
(8)   T.S. Eliot
(9)   Hart Crane
(10)   Langston Hughes
(11)   Elizabeth Bishop
(12)   Robert Lowell
(13)   Sylvia Plath

This Chapter asks the fanciful question: What if each of these poets wrote about the blues in their own distinctive style? The following thirteen poems were written as a series of answers—or perhaps as a series of blues-related questions.

Blues Like The Tides

WALT, WALT

Walt, Walt, and more Walt.

Walt with the American blues.

Walt taking on the melancholy
left over from Mayflower-stalks
and the flowers which bloomed
on the battlefields of the un-Civil War.

Walt, Walt,
now they've named high schools
after you. You? With so much
anti-gay ugliness
in the Walt Whitman lockerroom?

Walt, Walt, we need you now, now
that songs are selfish demands
and compassion's only contraband...

High school greed for brand name duds?
Ball game victories filling eyes with blood?

High schools full of electronic surf?
High schools where the grass is turfed?

High schools named for compassion personified?
High schools only true to the falsified?

Walt, Walt, we need you now more than then,
now, please, write us clean with compassion's art,
Walt, Walt, now that greed burns ragged holes
in pockets in pants, in pockets of hearts.

BUZZ FORCE

I heard that Fly—buzz—
Buzz the Blues—
The Table-cloth's color—
The blue-nosed News—

Like weary Notes
From a hurt Guitar—
Like—the Life Force— trapped
In a sealed-up—Jar—

Like Energy flowing
In rooted Flower—
Like Minutes crying
Through a sad-blue hour—

I heard his Buzz—
Deep as soaking Shower—
He buzzes his Blues
When he hears—ours—

THE FINE PRINT OF MY PEACE

Here in my
peaceloving room,
I see shadows sweeping
like death's broom
across my splintered desk—

I know that
eversweeping gloom
is not only on
my desk or tomb—
it's in my splintered chest.

Shadows mark
all my creations,
mark all my poems
of warring nations,
mark conflict in my inner selves.

I project out
from sniper eyes
so many shadows
which forever lie
on spines on my inner shelves.

The blues and I will
only sign a treaty
when they put their mark
on the fine print
of my peace.

BLACK YANG BLUES

A blackbird poemed a foreign tongue
outside my window way outside
my inner window too far inside
to measure in meters

I am unfamiliar with the lyric
sounded out there
so strange in here

I heard in my head pressed to white
pillow black-feathered order

All is artificial in my bed
till the poem of a bird
sings out the art
to my blank sheets

I was allsleep on a
laundered yin pillow
till I heard that bird
singing out the awakened
blank yang blues.

PLUM COLORS

Plums

so   much
        depends
on   the

reds they imply

on   the

blues they share

Plums

so   much
        depends

on   them

when they have the reds

they have the blues

FRAGMENT OF A CANTO FOR ST. ELIZABETH

...oh no...no...
...I no longer talk in here
of Dante and the resurrected
Roman Empire.
I lived in a vibrant Italy once,
now the only thing in italics
is the mocking word *asylum...*

It hums, *lum, lum, dum, dum...*

Every day I once knew
as Springloaded
has become just another
numbing remembrance
of the 5th century Fall...

I am struck hard,
struck dumb,
struck with shock,
lum. dum, lum, dum...

St. Elizabeth,
I'd ask you to pray for me,
if I only believed in you,
and only believed in me,
melum, medum...

BROOKLYN JACKIE

Take me out to the ballgame,
Brooklyn Jackie.
I wear the tricorn
for your independence...

LITTLE SNORING

Little Snoring, sleepy houses,
do you, crowned with Elizabethan thatch,
dream of the flowers of the American May?

THE WAKE

The stern of the ship,
the agitated wake,
water calling oh-so strong,
there are better bridges in the deep
than any suspension above.

ENOUGH LIGHT TO READ THE WEARY BLUES

Harlem, is there *here*,
I mean right *here*,
still enough light to read
the weary blues?

Harlem, is there here
enough blue electricity
to glow in the darkling soul?

I mean, when that Statue,
the one carrying a torch
for the blues,
takes to blowing
another American fuse?

THE GROWN-UP WAITING ROOM

The room is scary lighted
and shallow.

A *National Geographic* is full
of loaded breasts.

I think of the nurturing milk
I had, waiting for the days
of grown-up cancer.

FURRY AMEN

Is nature stinking chaos?
Are there garbage cans
of it in human nature?

So what? So be it.

Skunks are thankful for our garbage.

Black and white and furry amen.

COMING HOME TO ASHES

Ovens for people
under starving duress
we hear of all the time—
over there.

Over here,
they are for roasting
a life ill-done.

Blues Like The Tides

CHAPTER FOUR

ZENCHANTMENT

AND WORD JAZZ

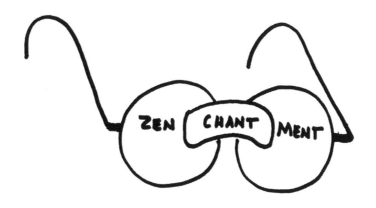

PART ONE: ECCENTRIC LEGACIES

NI TSAN

His houseboat glides,
glides on, glides over the inky river.

For thirty-seven years,
he feasted with social demands
and let his reclusiveness
almost starve.

Now the smile is happier,
and the painting delicious.

Now-gliding on a hermit's houseboat,
and now-watching the wake,
his mind is now-filled with
the now-joy of reclusiveness.

His society is the brush,
and his steady hand glides on,
making new wakes through dry paper.

The society of the brush:
the most reliable rudder
of a confirmed anchorite.

Now.

IN SPITE OF ITS SAINTLY ARMY

Just listen to that bridge
with its stiff squadron of saints,
and you just might hear again
Kepler's improvised variations
on the theme of the spheres...

He was crossing it
when it came to him
that the universe was not
what so many rigid holy men
wanted it to be.

A lot of firm believers
back then heard his variations
with a lot of stone ears.

But just listen to the history
that bridge recalls.

In spite of its saintly army,
it will always provide safe passage
for Bohemian astronomers
with minds free of any
stone cold haloes.

A CARELESS RIBBON

a careless ribbon, some errant lace
blurred lip gloss on her smiling face
the rustle of Julia's untucked shirt
the liquification of her dancing skirt

these brave vibrations fill
each errant and untucked line
and I wish some liqui-julia
could vibrantly enliven mine

here I smell a perfumed tune
in this dull-thudded noon—
a poem sings the melody of surprise
when you hear it with Herrick's eyes

BLAKE'S JEREMIAD

Chimneys in Blake's London
were cleaned by small boys
used as if they were brushes.

Their growth was purposely stunted
so they'd fit in narrower places
than cathedrals or houses of Parliament.

Blake died singing
and his last song could have been
a psalm, but I think
it was more likely a Jeremiad...

For it was not unlike Blake
to give his dying breath
to rail against an Empire
which looked upon child abuse
with all the empathy
of a chimney clogged with soot.

AN ECCENTRIC LEGACY

*"One misty, moisty morning
when cloudy was the weather,
I chanced to meet an old man
clo-thed all in leather."
--Anonymous*

Old Ben the Leather Man
didn't say much,
but, when he did,
it stayed with you,
like a thick-layered
saying from a leather oracle.

"There is a story
about my great, great,
and lots of more greats
Granddad, who once said
something magical.
There is not a day goes by
that I don't think about it."

He reached under the flap
of leather which covered
his hermit's face...

Near as I could tell,
I'm the only one he talked to
when I walked out from town
to give him some sandwiches
and rum.

I could hear him scratching
a hidden beard as he
continued thoughtfully.

"Back in colonial times,
it seems there was this argument,
and a hum-dinger it was...
Some colonists over to Portsmouth
already had the tar boiling
and the feathers plucked
for the King's taxman."

He moved the face cover
up a little more
from the hidden mouth,
so I could hear him
the better.

Only time I saw him do it,
except to wash down
the ham and cheese
with a swig of rum.

"There were angrier
than a gang of hornets,
when their nest is hit
with a sharp stick...

Chapter Four

So, then my really great Grand-dad
stands right up to
the lead nest-banger,
and here's what he said:
Hiss the flamingo."

"What?"

"That's it, all right,
Hiss the flamingo..."

He removed his face cover
entirely, a gesture of incredible
and unexpected trust.

I was touched,
and suddenly knew
he liked me more
than just because
I brought him
good food and better rum.

None of the hermits I helped
ever paid me that kind
of compliment.

"I don't have no clue
what it means neither,
but I know it worked."

"How?"

"Well, the lead agitator
started to laugh so hard
it became infectious.
The crowd lost its
momentum and they all went
to the pub instead."

"Did that really happen, Ben?"

"Must've.
It's the only thing
in my family legacy
worth a Goddamn.
If all the rest of my family
had been hissin' flamingoes
and not angry wasps,
I might not be
living in the woods
with a flap over my face."

MELVILLE'S LIGHTHOUSE

He's always in the literary lighthouse,
a reclusive keeper of constant light.

His ears are shells, constantly sounding
the roar of failure, cause even
the shells seem to know
his new book sold
only a few pathetic copies...

His hurt ego is whale-sized,
but he bears no grudge
against his publisher's
pasty frown of disappointment.

It was worth the writing.

And who knows, maybe someday
Moby Dick itself will become a lighthouse
to save some ship caught in
the dark waters of human folly.

RICH BEYOND AVARICE

"...the last twenty years...
Bentley lived alone
poor in worldly goods,
even to the verge of distress,
but rich beyond avarice..."
--First Supplement to
--The Dictionary of American Biography

This one thing we know
about his American biography:
the crystalline snow he loved
was never a drug.

Snowflake Bentley didn't have to wait
for any dealer other than
the Vermont winter
to deliver the goods...

The discoverer of new frontiers
in the winter air at home,
he didn't need to kill buffalo
or condescend to Buffalo Soldiers
to manifest his destiny.

His idea of American expansion
fell like a wonder from the sky.

His camera captured the essence
of American curiosity
and the freedom of nature
to express herself
in pursuit of the happiness
of infinite variety.

A SMALL BIOGRAPHY OF EZRA POUND
ON WALT WHITMAN'S FERRY

Crossing over to Brooklyn
once again, once again
feeling multitudes
in the single song of the self.

If you listened to
the white-whispered waves,
displaced by the hippopotamus
of the Brooklyn Ferry
taking its rhythmic bath,
you could hear the voice
of a good gray poet...

And the voice confirmed
the Poundian dictum:
"Pull down thy vanity."

The old boat docked.

It really was a lot different
than Walt had hoped for.

Faces of the vain
stuck to the windows
of shiny cars;
too many smiles of usury
on those helping themselves
to the smug shore.

LIKE A FRAME OF FILM

He carried his sensitivity
on his sleeve like an indelible stain.

And that insidious thrill
some get from making themselves
feel better at another's expense
repulsed him so much more
than all the spilled blood
of the War.

The night of the peacetime hunter
had as many hateful fingers
as the fist of a psychopath,
as it fell on him, here in the dark...

Sitting in yet, and yet, and yet
another darkened theatre,
he watched the Vice-President
facefill yet another
peacetime newsreel.

He could feel himself
being blistered once again,
like a frame on film
caught in the projector too long.

James Agee died oh so shortly
after that, his heart attacked
by a peacetime hunter.

VETERANS OF INNER WARS

(For Zora Neale Hurston)

And, what of those inner spaces,
filled with vacancies and lots?
She *crawled through sorrow's kitchen,
and licked clean all the pots.*

And she followed disappointing stars,
a wise woman who traveled afar.
She fell deep in jagged wells,
but that's where the saviors are...

And she traded all for foolscap,
and awoke to groundless dreams.
She witnessed her gifted soul
come apart at its inseams.

No stranger to foreign conflicts,
she searched out the firmament's scars,
knowing well no medals were awarded
to the Veterans of Inner Wars...

PART TWO: KEROUACIAN BEATITUDES

EVER-BEATING BEATITUDES

Kerouac asserted over and over
the term *beat* was not superficial.

He may as well have been Cassandra,
when her jazz was too far out
to be believed.

The papers only carried news
of slovenly youths in berets
beating borrowed bongos.

No, No, No,
Cassandra-Kerouac asserted,
it means empathy for the shell-shocked,
the beaten down with forty-yard stares
in their blood-tired eyes.

Few cared what *beat* really meant,
though not for the Cassandra telling:
we must all become more pluralistic,
more open to multiplicity,
more kind to the disinherited,
or our domesticated easy chairs
will crack under our overweight
condescension...

Who listens to an improvising prophet
when he jazz-mouths a riff
you don't want to hear?

Kerouac was concerned that America
was sick to the bone
if it could produce
such hard-hearted fools.

Those who listened at all
sermonized that the beat poets
had no values.

They were concerned that America
was sick to the bone
if it could produce
such soft-hearted fools.

Meanwhile, in the operating room,
Dr. Babbitt had prevailed,
and the ever-beating beatitudes
were immediately scheduled
for major heart surgery.

*=the beat jazzman takes on
the flannel dance of gray death=*

it's the fifties in America,
and the only light that gets out of
the innards of the flannel men
is gray, gray, gray....

the organization man
goes home to eat his gray dinner
on his polished vanity table,
while the multicolored jazz man
riffs away the improvised night...

*...gonna take a sentimental journey gonna take it four or five times
cause everything i do i try four or five times and when i die wont be
goodbye cause im gonna try to do it four or five times aint now nothing
like they used to be there used to be jobs in the war factories now
there are piece factories humming a flannel dance for gray men whos
jizz is gray-wise and jazz-wise even duller gray and gee whiz the
cheese whiz has gone off with his secretary and you can't run him up
the pole-wise to see if any gray body will salute hoagies dust on the
big star rising taint long for day thatll put an end to the gone jazz
night...*

it's the fifties in America
and a different kind of light
is also getting out—
it is a healing jazz balm
for an untended wound
that is turning more and more gray.

WHAT THEY WERE AFTER

Plastic has two
contrary meanings.

The beat poets railed
against the first—
there was something so ugly
about a suburban countertop
fixed in mortgaged space.

No, what they were after
was as plastic, that is as freeform,
as a hilltop blessing
gently delivered in kind vernacular...

Freeform for the meek,
not fixed for the rich.

What were they after?

Let's say it was plastic surgery
for the plastic headed.

A LOWELL OFFERING

They once asked Faulkner
why he didn't leave Mississippi.

The answer was simple:

The material is too good.

Kerouac did leave Lowell,
but he packed a lot of good material
in his rucksack.

You can go there and still see
things like this in the laundromat:

FOR SALE
and hardly never been sat on:
easy, boy, it's an Easy Boy—
paid $300—
yours for a hundred—
if your ass fits,
sit on it....

A pilgrimage to Kerouac country:
on the floor near the bulletin-tacked board,
a crumpled donut box, now frosting-less.

No donuts left—
frosting all gone—
as empty as an unfilled cavity
deep in one's heart...

The material is still good
in this Kerouacian country,
but it's time for me to hit
the frostingless road,
back anywhere
but an Easy Boy home.

If your ass won't fit,
get it on the road...

JAZZ MONTAGEFEST

New/ port/ fifty/ six
and it's a new take
on the flavors of America.

It's montagefest,
and Patti-windowed cute-doggies,

and Joe monotoned points of order,
and John Foster's speeches—
what's his last name again?—

oh, right, dull—
none of them, none
can find the antidote
to the recent jazz infestage...

For the *Newport Rhode
Island Jazz News*
won't take any advertising
from the Pavlovian
Tin Pan Company,

any more, cause it
only tells the story of
how jazz is

reinvigoratin' vanilla life,
granting chocolate liberty,
and busting out all over the sky
cause jazz enthusiasts are pursuing
strawberry happiness...

It's enough to melt
every pint-sized portion
of the American ice dream.

BEAT CHIASMUS

Death   stills
installment   debts.

But wait, there's more, cause
it's important to remember
whose hearts are chanting,
and what they are chanting,
and why they are chanting it,
and, anyway, here's the beat chiasmus
to balance the debts of installment death:

Beat   hearts
chant   being.

THE CODE-BREAKERS

Enigma Code.

Who won the war?

You can make a good case
for the codebreakers.

Homefront.
Sentences sentenced to
plain straightforward
pragmatic down-to-business
English with a
MAKE MONEY spin...

Who's winning the domestic war?

You can make a good case
the Beats are at least trying.

SOME MORE OF THE DHARMA

There are spaces
in breathing
where desire
for approval
and for anxious
getting and spending
recede into
silence.

Death doesn't
know these spaces,
not only because
he is unable to hold
his breath,
but also because
he is always
in over his bonehead
with too much overtime...

You can breathe in and out,
breathe in lifesaving rhythms,
breathe out as if death matters
don't matter.

And as if the sound of a silent bell
were more than enough...

OUT OF THE WRITING

swollen droplets
drop cats
drop dogs
in water sheets

the poet's drenched
but won't come in
out of the writing

OFF THE BLUE HIGHWAY,
KEROUAC FINDS A LIVE END

So, here, in America,
where the sun
can be paroled
from a sentence
of nightly solitaire,
let's come off
the whitmanesque road
and the eisenhower rood
and hum the live end
which goes round and round
and never square
round and round
every which word way
and comes out a blues
here and now and then
deepbottomed...

PART THREE: GINSBERG'S EPISTLES

WILL THE CIRCUIT STAY UNBROKEN?

All the best minds of their generation
drifted aimless and on the prowl,
seeking fresh verse and verification
for any poet unafraid to howl.

And will beat circuits stay unbroken
in the dark sun and hot rain?
There's a better poem a-coming
in the highway of our brains.

They took every unmarked exit,
absorbing life like thirsty towels.
They took every unmapped back road
and found places with unknown vowels.

Ginsbergesque and Kerouackian,
coining currency for the loins of realm—
they jumped every shape of every ship
when conformity took the helm.

THE DOUBLE EFFECT OF A WATERFALL

In the Jerseyed dawn,
a grown-up son and his father
slid pieces of paper
containing complementary poems
down an ancient waterfall
of splashing companionship.

The father's fountain pen
had flowed with seasoned resonations,
but the son's carried shadows
of the leaves of a Buddha tree.

They saw the same waterfall,
but the father was thinking of
the Indian for whom it was named,
while the son was thinking
of the energy of Indian poetry.

Father and son left the waterfall,
taking two entirely different directions.

Allen Ginsberg's father
went back to teaching
Civil Disobedience in Patterson High,
but he did it a little too obediently
for his son, who went back
to a Manhattan Walden to poem it.

Every waterfallen line
was dedicated to Siddhartha.

ROCKWELLIAN DECONSTRUCTION
ON THE UPPER WEST SIDE

An expensive book
of Norman Rockwell paintings
graced the window
of a used bookstore,
telling of a home-cooked utopia
far from the Upper West Side.

But here we have a guy
Rockwell never
would have painted.

He's sitting on
broken chair
by the subway
entrance across
from the bookstore.

Seems he was so
overwhelmed by the
large number of passengers
that he couldn't
expose himself
in the normal way.

Too much work
to wear a raincoat
and have to
open and close it
so many times...

Instead he just stayed
sitting down
with a big hole
cut in the crotch
of his tattered pants.

The window advertising Norman
also contained a clear reflection
of a pervert too lazy
to practice his trade
with much enthusiasm.

THE REAL INTENTION

Inside the club called *The Id*,
an honest jazz singer finds
the truth latent in a riff.

Here takes place a discovery
of jazz psychology:
Here is what Freud implied
but never stated:
scats of the jazz tongue
show the real intention
of a subconscious riff.

ALMOND FLAME

Where is the space
between beat contraction
and beat expansion?

The apostrophe
that makes
the 'finite
infinite?

There's an almond flame
in every meditating candle.

That almond flame
resists anything associated
with packaged nuts.

THE SUNSET'S SMILE

We are told in the West
to avoid the pathetic fallacy,
but this isn't always
the best way
to see the sunset.
Pathos is everywhere,
as any western Buddhist
soon finds out.
If cloud can cry
the language of thunder,
why can't the sunset smile
the silence of lightning?

GINSBERG'S LIVE SEA

It's *as if*—

as if you set out
on a long as-if journey...

as if down a long as-if dead sea...

as if you made it to a port
where a forgotten library
was buried in the as-if sand...

As if you fell
into an underground cave
of hidden memories...

and *as if* you found there
a different bible

and *as if* it gave you
new vowels
for your as-if
live sea prayer...

GRADULATION WITH GRACE

The once parallel tracks
of a youth too sensitive to live
and a middle-aged poet
too energized to mellow

meet, meet

in an unexpected reversal
of high school expectations:

suddenly new tunes,
ones without pomp

ones without pomp
which freely grant
degrees and degrees

degrees and degrees of
grace in every
circumstance.

APHORISMS IN THE LININGS OF CLOUDS

The clouds are the gods of the idle.

Wait. Did I hear that right?
Isn't it more like this?

If your thoughts don't move
as freely as a cloud,
your idolatry stays far worse
than the idleness you condemn.

# # #

Clouds never stay home.
Nor should we.
We are, like they,
the exiles of the skies...

# # #

From the point of view
of Diogenes looking at the sky:
Any cloud can be greater
than Alexander on the march.

WILD CARD IN A FIXED DECK

Everything were are taught
is the equivalent
of a fixed deck...

1st card, 2nd card, 3rd card...

...a predestination
of exact number and suit...

4th card, 5th card.

...As if a life of
unnumbered and unsuited ways
were just what law calls arbitrary...

cardandcardandcard...

...just what law calls capricious...

cardandcard...

...Better, much better,
to think of the writer
dissenting against predestination
as the wild card
in that fixed deck...

...as the wild card
dissenting against

...the non-pulsing heart...

...the unfaceted diamond...

...the law of the clubhouse...

...and the burial spade...

card, card, wild...

PART FOUR: BEAT APOCALYPSES

OVERTURE TO A DYSFUNCTIONAL ADDING MACHINE

Suppose your childhood is like some
overture full of correct answers
from your father's adding machine...

and suppose there is no ribbon of melody,
only black repeating numerals,
black and pitted
as the pupil of William Tell...

and suppose you suspect
the target isn't the apple...

THE BEAT POET TAKES ON HIS BATHROOM MIRROR

"Perfect is the enemy of good."

Mirror, mirror, on the medicine wall,
give me more some more
of that kind of medication.

"OK," the mirror mocked,
"you're a perfect literary outlaw,
good at balding rapidly.
Can that be your hairline
that's receding faster
than conventional civilization?"

The mirror reflected a face
thinking hard for a response.

"Better than the alterative."

"Oh yeah, what's that?"

"An advancing hairline."

THE BEST LINE IN
THE TEN COMMANDMENTS

The lifeforce is forever
watching an extra
say the best line
in the movie version
of *The Ten Commandments.*

Charleton Moses is forced
into a muddy ditch
and taskmasked to make bricks
for the Pharaoh's version
of Sinai, that is, a pyramid.

"You must be new to the pits."

That's what makes a stone structure
less pompous than its builder wants:
unintended humor between
the commanding stones.

UNDER THE BRIDGE

Sleep well, but remember those
who must sleep under a bridge.

Sleep well, but remember those
who must sleep under the bridge
of a nose looking down on them.

NOT MUCH TALLER
THAN NAPOLEON

In the shank of the apocalyptic evening,
a drugged poet has again
seen his work knock down
a third of the sky.

Not much taller than Napoleon,
he senses another third
will soon fall right into
his junkie brain.

How can you help thinking
of your own cold-turkey Waterloo
when the other third of the sky
is poised and ready to hit you
with its short end?

THE LAND OF COCKAIGNE

He loves the road, for its rite is passage.
His leg tendons pull for some change.
He is restless as a nursing-homed nomad
listening to *Home on the Range*.

He's got to jump good neighbor fences.
He can't wag stuck in the impound.
He can't stand for standing still,
and can't sit on the shifting ground.

He's a fighter for constant change
Fight or flight means *fight* for *flight*.
The Land of Cockaigne is calling
and he'll be gone 'fore the falling night.

CUTTING THROUGH THE NEWS

Cutting some cardboard on newspaper,
he discovered something.

The news had a brand new meaning
if you read down through it
rather than conventionally across.

Reading headlines this way
confirms *Man Bites Dog*,
especially if that dog
is the personification
of a any man who refuses
to learn new tricks.

BALLAD OF THE THIN-AIRED MAN

I'm a man who breathes in sorrow,
I've seen the ashes in every blaze.
I've headed for some small town plot,
where I was grown, but hardly raised.

I don't know how I got this fallen,
I thought I had divorced despair.
I only know just one thing, Darling:
what keeps us from tragedy is only thin air.

I'm a man who breathes in sorrow,
I swear there's ashes in every blaze.
I swear to you by the earth's dark tunnel,
that I was born, but can't be raised.

BURY HIM STANDING

Going native in America—
it's as if our own Native Americans
were as foreign to General Motors
as natives of the East Indies.

The Beatnik did not
die standing pat.

No, he did not die rich,
except that while alive
he made over 100,000 ideas
a year...

So, he's earned something more
than the richest man
in the graveyard.

He's earned the right
to be buried standing.

He's earned that right,
'cause all his life
he spent far too much time
on his beaten-up knees.

UNNUMBERED COMING

It all still waxes,
unsealed
and unnumbered.

Somewhere
someone
somehow
found some
Redemption
left behind
by someone
misunderstood
misremembered
and misrepresented.

The first and second
wane.

The unnumbered still waxes.

Blues Like The Tides

CODA

DON'T KNOW WHAT IT MEANS

IMPROVISING RIDDLE: INNER HARP

I'm a treat for fast fingers
when they're a-razz-a-tazzin',
tappin' out tunes
on my inner harp,
when they set it re-
soundin'

some'll tell ya
no is at my end
but if you play me right
all the yessin' night
there's no end
to the joy I give
to them with caressin' fingers

when the harp in my chest
reaches out to the beat in yours,
who am I when
the blues touch home?

THE MAN WHO CLAIMED
HE INVENTED JAZZ

Piano.

Bring it back back
back to new whore
or leans house,
back to me jelly
roll morton

my rollin' ring fingers
on aphro dees siac
keyboard invented
jas jass jaz jazz

its story is my
ville way before
the navy chased the blues
up the river
I swear by the diamond
in my tooth
I put the gleam
in jas yas jazz yazz...

inventive jazz
on flat keys
the forgotten elephant
gave his sharps for
the flatlands here

back back back
in drumming old
rhythmrich Africa

I me myself I
in my major fingers
and minor keys
unlocked richrhythm
fat or lean
jazz a man tazz
I me all by
my o my
self

nuff said
now boys
re member me
when you play
in joints
deep in marrow
jazz jelly and jam
to your wild heartstent

IMPROVISING RIDDLE: BELLY TO BELLY

When you hold me in your hand,
we make love belly to belly

I have an hour-glass figure
and I love it
when you plug me in

Who am I to fill up your belly
with desire for
such hunger-pane music?

JINX'S TUNE

I'll always remember
Jinx and her electric guitar.

She only knew one riff,
which she played over and over,
but somehow it was inspiring
each time, even though
she played it the same way,
as a bird will sing out
his signature tune.

Musicians called it
"Jinx's Tune."

Jinx played it the same
each time, but somehow
she made you think of variations
when it nestled in your ear.

She was nicknamed
for her bad luck,
but she played the blues
for good.

Unlucky at cards and love,
she found recognition
in a single song….

It brought up enough
from deep inside
to produce a genuine smile
from her and the listener.

# # #

She was tiny and quiet,
and there was nothing to her
when she wasn't playing
her small tune.

But when she did,
she became very largely alive.

The comfort it gave her
she gave to you too.

Whenever I remember her
playing her tune
on her beat-up electric,
I always imagine it stays
where it should be:
plugged in to my ear.

IMPROVISING RIDDLE: NO MORE LUMBERIN'

Who do you think I am when I tell you in life
my tree was silent, but in death
my curved wood sings?

Believe me I ain't lumberin'
when you wrap your
rappin' fingers round my neck,
and I ain't chokin' neither
when I hit hard
the base bottom bass line...

IN MACYS THE CASH REGISTERS

He ordered Bass ale
and told a Christmas joke.

It was funny,
it was sad,
it was both,
a jazz joke kinda
bad, ale bass, bad ass:

A kid steals the statue
of the baby Jesus
and writes a note to God saying
"If you ever want to see
your son again, give me a new
bicycle for Christmas.

#

in macys the cash
registers quarters
of torn holly

splitting snooze alarm
zigzagedly tells
come Christless morning
all are once again
going to malls
and buyin up
the brokeline bridge
and linebrook farm

taxispeeding by
pieces on earth
yelloh ho ho ho
stopping to pick up
reindeer with weary hooves

empty sack
on broken mantle
lost all crisp mass

no balaam
but lots of milk
in talkinglasses

if your plastic baby
to see jesus
comb again
send bankershours

Coda

no pole ice
in macys
windowpain

joke kid
got ransom cycle

grand centralsoul
back in feedingstation.

IMPROVISING RIDDLE: SKIN RATTLIN'

Who am I
when you rattle my skin,
when you tap my head
and I make rhythm
without one thought
of any kind of headache?

QUARTER IN THE WATER

I was drumming on the table
cause the waitress seemed
to delight in ignoring us.

What did she have against us?

It was just about a perfect night,
but not for her...

We were percussion/discussing
acoustic vs. electric,
blues *vs.* jazz,
but not that there
was always a *vs.*
between them,
in fact maybe never,
cause the two fit together
like two bits,
a cool non-shave
and a beat haircut...

She finally brought us
two water glasses,
which she plunked down,
but still no menus.

No matter,
the jazz group was
only two tables away
and was combo-ing the night,
by which I mean
turning our night-out
into a rich combination
of noir notes and
bright musical gleams.

And I was happily drumming
the table along,
in bluesjazz jazzblues
rhythms, hms, hms...

Coda

Then I saw a look
of electric shock
on my girlfriend's face
as she took a glance
into her water glass.

George Washington
was looking back at her,
because there was a quarter
nearly drowning
in the bottom.

"Hope George can hold his breath..."

"It must be evidence of
a failed attempt to throw a quarter
across the Delaware."

"Yeah, but is he reviewing
his whole life?"

"If he drowns, will
the cherry tree still stand?"

She laughed and was about
to order cherries-jazz-jubilee
when the, *if* the
waitress ever came back...

I drummed an accompaniment
to some jazz thinking:

*What if this whole experience
were muse-ical, a be-bopping way
of telling us to improvise—
to think up the name
of a new jazz combo,
or a maybe give new life
to a familiar proverb?*

Now my brain was drummin' with
the *Quarter in the Water Glass,*
featuring that *wild saxman
with the compound eyes*
who made *the Ointment Club*
buzz as if he were
flying with the bumble bee...

"Quick, finish your water."

I quickly drank up my whole glass.

She took my emptied glass
and poured the water
from her own into it.

George, very wet, was rescued...

The band was taking a break.

We quickly decided to take one too.

It was OK, the music
had told me.

No need to get angry,
especially if you looked
at the whole experience
from compound eyes...

So, it was Presidents' day
for our waitress,
as we left her
a dry Lincoln on a crisp bill,
and a wet Washington on a coin
saved from drowning.

A wild proverbial sax
was irresistibly
calling out to us
from over at
the Ointment Club.

IMPROVISING RIDDLE: PHONIN' LINES

Give me a call,
and I'll return it
on a hopping line.

The wind may bloooow
harder than I can,
but I make the wind
into jazz
and no wind never done that
for me.

I need human lips
to make me jive,
and I can jump the wind,
whenever he just blows
the same old standards.

BIRD HUMMING HOME

sax-o-phone us
all the humming way
home

humming home
where the sax heart is

humming bird homing bird
coming humming
on heartening home

Coda

flying yards above
the prison yard bones

sax-o-phone, fly us
into the wild blue music
making up the sky

all the way home
from a blues view eye...

IMPROVISING RIDDLE: QUALITY NOT STRAINED

We need this kind instrument the most
the most
when blues are at high tide
when we narrow art so it can't look wide
when we give up on a spiritual guide
when poets fixate on suicide
when beat attitudes die on the mountain side
when jazz stays out and not in -side

then that's when
we need this kind instrument
the most:

what is it?

the bluesman said it best
when he sang:

Everybody's crying "Mercy, Mercy"
but they don't know what it means...

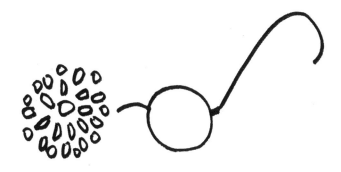

ABOUT THE AUTHOR

STEPHEN C. SHAW is the retired Director of Administrative Rules for the State of New Hampshire. He retired at 50, and has been writing, painting, playing slide guitar, and traveling ever since. He lived abroad for four years, and has taught courses on the poetry of the blues in both Prague and Cambridge, England. He has written several books of poetry based on his travel experiences, including *New Life Lines in the Palms of My Hands*. He now lives in Harrisburg, PA.

NOTE

The text illustrations and the painting on the cover are by the author.

A CD of several of the songs in *Blues Like the Tides* is available by contacting:

Stephen C. Shaw
stephencraigshaw@yahoo.com
or
books@parisburgpublishing.com

Special thanks to Walter Dolen for making it all possible.

Blues Like The Tides

Made in the USA
Charleston, SC
03 March 2011